Christ in the Pizza Place

poetry

Clyde Rose

Christ in the Pizza Place

poetry

Clyde Rose

Jesperson Publishing

Jesperson Publishing
39 James Lane
St. John's, NF Canada
A1E 3H3

Cover and Book Design: *Sue Wright and Ray Fennelly*
Printing: *Sam Cicciarella, Jesperson Press*

Printed in Canada.

Canadä

We acknowledge the financial support of the Government of Canada through the Book Publishing Industry Development Program (BPIDP) for our publishing activities.

Canadian Cataloguing in Publication Data

Rose, Clyde, 1937–

    Christ in the pizza place

    ISBN 0-921692-94-3

I. Title.

PS8585.072543C5 1999   C811'.54   C99-950244-1
PR9199.3.R5878C5 1999

Christ in the Pizza Place is dedicated to my father and mother, who by their example taught me about love (especially of Newfoundland), friendships and loyalty. To all those who are friends and those I love I also dedicate these poems in gratitude for the many times—and in so many places around the world—I was welcomed as if I were arriving home.

Clyde Rose
St. John's, NF

Table of Contents

The Tap Dancer

My God how he could dance
his feet tapped the floor
like a dying flatfish
beating its life out
on a wet stagehead.

March Morning in New York

for brother Max

A cold wind cuts through these canyons
not warmed by billions of neon lights
still flashing night's brightness
in the early morning dawn.

On this same day
fifty-eight years ago
my elder brother was born...
my mother waited upstairs
in a cold bedroom
for the arrival of the midwife.
Grandmother Coley
clothed in a long black dress
a black shawl wrapped
round her head and shoulders
was an ominous figure
as she trudged through
the snow to perform her role.
So many times, she thought,
and yet the woman bore no boys.
Maybe today, she mumbles.
Mothers and children too
steal glances through
curtained kitchen windows
as she makes her way
there on that March day.

From within the bedroom
the cold wind can be heard
whistling through seams and cracks.
Down in the harbour
husbands and fathers return
from winter's banks
sou-westers white with slush
knots of saltwater coiled
in lumps around their necks.
Voices muffled in vapour cold
cheeks like red leather burnt with salty winds
eyebrows strung with frosty pearls
back and muscles fire-red
from pain of labour.
I need a son he thought.
The ache and pain piercing
his winter body like needles
to the brain.

Casting her dark black shawl
upon the trunk in the corner
she quietly goes about her work
amidst the scream of pain.
She orders
hot water, clean cloths
and wipes the perspiration
from the brow
giving at considered intervals

words of comfort—
Be patient now, my dear,
it will all be over bye and bye.
A southwest wind
turns the corner of the house
just before dark—
its shriek covers Fox Island
and muffles the sounds
of a boy-child
brought to life.
A smile breaks the austere face
behind the black shawl—
and down in the stage
baiting up yet another tub of gear
he pauses for a moment
beats his arms around his body
feels the blood returning
heaves his shoulders back
as a new strength
enters his soul.

Maiden Rodney

A southern light shines
through the windows
of the shed
where his nimble fingers stroke
the timber,
gunwales,
bow and risings,
into shape.

A rodney is being born.

Her contours resemble
the curves and warmth
of a Newfoundland maiden.

The flange of her bow,
the gentle sweep of her stern
give her the symmetry
of a mussel shell
as she sits
gently on the water.

Feather-light she'll meet,
lap;
and part

saltwater waves
like a lover caressing another.

When strong winds blow
and heavy seas
attempt to drive her down
she'll recoil with passion
ride to the top
like a turr on the lop
where she sits,
triumphant,
Queen of her rodney realm.

❧

Trinity

for Tom Maybee

Town of rich West Country
merchants
who pretended they loved
the place
while people laboured
loving the saltwater,
cliffs, coves and stubborn spruce
that grew in granite seams
where trees ought not
to grow....
Such is our heritage—
saltwater and brine
fog in our marrow
axes and hammers
in our hands
—high-tech half-hitches
networking our lives
in our landwash home
—in love with thole-pins
tawts and piggins
unmindful all too much
of ourselves
and the distant urban horizon—
plowing on bows under
seeking the Newfoundland lund.

Newfoundlander on a Late Night Toronto Bus

He rolled on board
with his Nova Scotian
friend of the night
much like the sea heaving
into a sheltered cove.
Somewhere out on the St. Clair West
bus platform
the driver sat with his mates
watching the clock
agonizingly creep round to departure time.
Back on board, Toronto's
haggards of the night sat silently waiting.
Too poor for cabs.
This was the last run and the wait
was always long.
Except for one this night.
A rare one. His sea-burnt eyes
caught their agony.
His free spirit
their pride.
And from his heart there came a song
whose roots lay deep in Celtic hills
of Ireland....

As I roved out one evening
all in the summertime.

A haggard looking Canadian gent
felt a surge of ancient spirit
and leapt from his seat to say:
"Aeh laddie you're like a breath
of heather over the highlands...."
It was all he said
as songs poured forth.
A Japanese Canadian removed
his boots
and leaned back
in new comfort
as if in gardens
filled with blossoms and quince
content forever.
All others, nondescript, sat transfixed,
hoping this too real dream
would never end.

it did
a thud
a smack
a footstep at the door
a grunt
a hiss of compression
a door slammed shut

The song stopped.

A new voice
began
Canadian born and bred
"Well let's put an end to this."
Leaving us puzzled
as to whether he meant
his night
his last bus run
or our song.

꧁꧂

John Thompson Is Not Listed

My sisters have gone home
to their husbands' beds
my aged mother, as always,
lies half awake in her room
her son has come home to visit
and tired as she is
she will not surrender to sleep

Outside, the Montreal night
sweats with summer heat
my father's body lies bleached
in the cool earth
his saltwater voice
only a memory

My friends are somewhere
in Newfoundland
at cottages, parties or beaches
far from this St. Luc tenement

I am too afraid
on this Montreal summer night
to open the doors of memory
rather I'll sit here, drink,
get tired
make some phone calls

insist
to the Bell Telephone supervisor
that the man
who taught me to read
Ayn Rand
Kazantzaskis
and Shakespeare
still lives
in a dirty little apartment
in L'acadie Estates

And if he doesn't
they have no business
removing his name
from our list
of friends
we call in the night

꧁꧂

Convergence

We are like twin stars
in the universe
with our long history
behind us—
only now
seeing each other's light—
only now
switching
from a parallel course
unto a converging one.

Each of us trembles
at the thought:
two stubborn, valiant hearts
exposing their nakedness
with fear of vulnerability
loss of pride
the horror
of being hypocritical.

Not us.
Not you.
Not me.
Never.

Let's let love
bring us together
and NASA-like slide
with the precision
of a spaceship
into one another's sphere.

❧

True to Type

A Czech border guard
as stunned as my arse
demands my passport—
puffed with power
he points to my luggage
mumbles about a visa
directs me off the train
away from my book
of Irish short stories
written by journalists
from the *Irish Times*
true to type

This policeman
picks me out on the train
a bearded man with a book
as his victim
he'll slaver tonight in his goulash
over my helplessness
in the semi-darkness
of the no-man's land frontier
between Germany and Czechia

Life is a strange old whore
one minute your soul
is in the bottom of your boot

the next—
you're soaring through
the milky way
Within an hour
I have found a nice hotel
the host of which phones
my hotel in Prague
to explain my delay

a nice bar
where the patrons
struggle with their English
to ensure that I travel
to the right town to get
my visa in the morning
a hot meal; some wine
and then to bed

I hear the roar of wind
and out of the swirl
comes a Czechian princess
whose mantle of golden hair
rolls in Rapunzel waves
down her back—
the wind subsides
to a gentle breeze
taking my hand she guides me
over the river
to a gentle spot

where she weeps for me
and vows to avenge my denial
from her country

She feeds me venison from the forest
and we drink jars of wine
in earthen cups
she beckons me to lie down
on bear skins
spread by an open oak fire
and keeps me warm til dawn

All through the night
the river gurgles
oak logs crackle in the fire
the milky way turns up the stage lights
and heaven's arena bursts forth
with music and song . . .
just before dawn
an old song sung a cappella
wafts in from a rocky island
in the Western Ocean.

I close my eyes to listen
to this familiar tune
and when the song ends
I wake and find her gone.

Hurtin' Poem

for Rex Brown

A Bavarian woman
bearing warm bread
came into my office
I promised you
this, she said,
some time ago
I, of course,
as with many promises
had forgotten
I rose
took the bread
gazed on its lovely colour,
felt its warmth
placed it on
my desk
turned and kissed her
on the cheek
and hugged her
hard
she felt like she had been
made
with the bread
in the oven
It's a happy day she said,
our friend made it

through the second hearing
She can be a Canadian now
she said
A Newfoundlander
I said
Oh yes, she said,
of course, a Newfoundlander
I looked from her deep brown eyes
to the light brown warm bread
the place felt
like my mother's kitchen
back home in Burgeo and
I felt like a boy in love

Lovers in the Lund

Words tumble around
in my head
like magic balls
setting off memories
what's your favourite word
I was asked the other night
lund, says I
unhesitatingly
just like that
magic balls tumble over
I hear
the voice of my father
get the dory narder, my son,
and paddle her over to the lun'
then quick as a flash
my mind tumbles
into another memory
walking up the moonlit road
over the naked windswept rocks
with my childhood sweetheart
where shall we go, she says,
with a voice full of love
and telltale cheeks
red under the moon
let's go lie in the lund says I
she smiles

the magic balls inside my head
crash into one another
like breakers
smashing on the rocks
of cliffs
where lovers lie above

Images

Words
from your mouth
dropping softly
like autumn leaves
to a fall ground.
The music of your voice
like a westerly wind
brushing a lonely island
off the Sou'West Coast
of Newfoundland.
Your hair
like the grass
on Fox Island beach
twirling and curling
around
in my memory.
Your presence
like a poem
a fresh breeze
in the harbour—
a torment to my heart.
Your beauty
like a winter storm
fierce, wild,
overwhelming—
a song to my soul.

Iceberg Heat

Great lovers
are like
majestic
Newfoundland
icebergs
they linger—
coming not just
for the winter
but the spring
and summer too—
they know something about
heat—

SLOW

heat

Black Coral

Part 1

Come dive with me
into the deep blue Cuban sea
and follow me down
into undersea coral gardens
where the fish are velvet
black, blue and gold
and pinnacles of coral growth
in mossy brown
stand out like the antlers
of a seasoned bull moose.

You have just one breath
to glide you to this garden
under the surface
where you must carefully sway
with the current
avoiding the jagged razor-
edged reefs
alert to unexpected movement
as fish dart in and out
from the murky, shadowy
grottos on the rocky bottom.

The light that comes from the sun
one hundred and forty-four billion

kilometres away
transforms the scene
into a virtual kingdom
under the sea.

It was in this primal soup
that life began
and may yet end.

Part II

Follow me down deep with Luis
master diver of the Caribbean.

In the evolutionary process
Luis is a marvel—
genetic development allows him
to live underwater for four minutes.

I watch him now as I glide
behind him in this coral haven
on a steady line of descent
his left arm behind his back,
his hand gracefully placed flat,
as if he were about to do a cotillion.
He pirouettes his body
along the coral dancefloor
filled with magic and light

and schools of fish
swaying in harmony
to a silent waltz
in this Vienna ballroom under the sea.
Luis reaches the ledge
beyond which is a
dark blue darkness.
He looks back
over his shoulder
with a thumbs up
to his partner.
This is the signal:
I'm OK—
carry on independently.

He tumbles over
into the darkness
in search of the black coral
twenty-five metres down
at another sunlit level.
I head back up
leaving a trail of pearly bubbles behind
as I exhaust my way
to the surface
lungs burning
shooting for the sunlight:
a desperate blow
a loving inhalation

and I'm back
in the earth's atmosphere again.
I've been gone one minute
it will be three more
before Luis returns.

Part III

I bob around waiting
on an empty ocean.
Down there somewhere
Luis seeks his quest—
the elusive black coral.
Man the challenger of nature
nature the nurturer of man—
putting him to his test
one minute, two minutes,
three minutes, four minutes.
How much longer and how much further
can the species go?
Perhaps a great gene
will click and clone with
Luis' and our species will once again survive
under the water.

Part IV

A fierce spout grabs my attention
a jet of spume shoots

sunward—
a mask, a head
then a hand brandishing
black coral in the sunlight.
Luis has risen.
I thrash my mortal way
to him in the water
to grasp his godly hand.

❧

Jamaican Man

for Rebecca

He sprung like a cat
out of the afternoon sunlight
smiling
his two front teeth like machetes
he took the heavier pieces of baggage
ran with them up the steps of the villa
as if they were toys
then he was gone

Later in the dark dark
of a Jamaican evening
his gardening and chores done for the day
he became the guard of the villa
on his head a woollen stocking cap
under his belt a long knife
responding to every noise in the night
pouncing from one corner of the villa
to another
his head a rainbow flash
against a black sky

Early one morning
long before the sun had risen
he took us up to his land in the mountains
where he grew green bananas, yams
we hairpinned our way up
through the villages

where people were already awake
gathered in groups
their soft voices drifting on the dawn air
—every now and then a shout—
finally when we entered his village
great growls of joy
as he extended his hand
from the car window
to greet friends
Yeah, man
Yeeaaahh

In the field
machete in hand
his lightning strokes
brought long leaves
and great green bundles of bananas
falling from the sky to the ground
cool drops of water rained down on us
as he slashed and swept his way
through the jungle of trees...

All of a sudden
he is in a crouch
on the ground — a shorter knife in hand
punching the dry rich soil
where pieces of yams are lying
a thief
—we gather it might be his son—
has taken his best yams

left the tops on the ground instead of burying them
so that they might grow again

His anger flares up,
his nostrils widen
he whirls the knife around
he looks at me
his eyes red with rage
and says as he arcs his knife
Sir, if I knew the man who took my yams
and did this I would cut his neck off

I believe him

Moments later
his anger quelled
he moves catlike
toward his load
filling his arms
with bunches of bananas and yams
—those that have not been stolen—
the sun shines on silver rivers of sweat
on his body
his eyes have lost their rage
he smiles his machete smile
and purrs

The land is good, boss, the land is good

Cutthroat

for Eli, my Inuit friend

From the window
of the twin otter
the shoreline below us
is lined with chipped ice
strung like broken pearls
around the elegant neck
of the frozen canyon
upwards and northwards
over the snow-covered
Kiglapaits
whose granite edges pierce the sky
like a giant pit saw.

From the top of the mountain
near Man of War peak
a sunlit river flows
to the sea
where the brown, barren
island of Cutthroat
sits in contrast
against a pearl white
frozen sea.
Alongside me sits Eli
an Inuit hunter
looking longingly down

at Nutak
a forsaken village
where his father and mother
were born.
On through the split peaks
that stand out like
a bishop's mitre—
suddenly the plane drops
as we pass over
jagged edges
where thousands of feet below
lie fjords filled
with a mix of local
and Arctic ice
white and turquoise.

The sun on water
light on white
—two suns—

A grey granite
and turquoise evening.

Live Art in Gros Morne

Outside my window at the bar
the gulls are having a windy
afternoon November frolic
darting, gliding, soaring,
plunging
in the picture frame
of these panes—
live art.
Some sit on the water
where they are hove up and down
against a dark deep green background
of Gros Morne hills.
The others,
perhaps they are younger,
swirl above them
against a backdrop
of blue sky and ivory sunset clouds.
There are thousands of wings
out there
and thousands of bodies
swooping and soaring
at top flight
in the same
window frame space.
They're going in all directions

up and down
over and across—
all this a part
of some strange harmony—
some supreme communication.
There's not even
a near miss
in the directionless traffic
in this world of wing and feather.
A collision would be an insult
to their dignity
of flight.

Paradise Found

for Pat Byrne

November is a strange time
to head out the bay.
Our earlier trips were made
when warm May winds blew
lobster was on the haul
we stayed on deck
pointing to the headlands
rocks and shoals
as our fathers did
so many times before.

The fall trip showed us new sights
recent lights that beckoned
from Paradise Head
where the graveyard sits
on a sloping hillside
above the sea
where a knarly old tree
marks the grave
where your Godfather
Jack Mulroney lies.

Sometime that night
many stories after we landed
Uncle Jack Lake sang

"Three Jolly Sailors."
It wasn't the song so much
as the singing of it
that struck us
with his head
buried in his hands
resting on the kitchen table
he looked like Rodin's
"The Thinker"
his saltwater dreams
pouring forth
in old melodies and rhythms.

Walking on the shore
with Marticott Island
in the background
I heard your voice
swell up around the harbour
—it probably echoed
all the way
to Little Paradise—
as you described
your mother's garden on the hill;
your father's command
to you in the rough seas
when the dory took on water:
—don't bawl b'y, bail—
A trail of memories

echoing up and down
Paradise Sound
friends opening up their treasure chests
of stories and songs
in November's cold air.

❧

Three Children Standing

Three children standing
by the landwash
their backs to us—

The blond haired child
on the left
has her head turned
she is not looking
at the object
in the water
she's looking down
her hands clasped
behind her back
she's holding her hands tight
she's trying to understand
but she's too young
she's probably crying
but we cannot see her face
she would not want us
to see her now
unhappy, bewildered, confused
all we see is the dark and light
checkered dress
with a white collar—
on her feet

cutoffs—
symbols of the poor

The tall boy in the middle
wearing jeans with braces
a striped t-shirt
is looking out
at the object
in the water
he has the stance
of the outport man
hip slung out
at an angle
it'll be that way
forever
it's the only way to talk
when you're down
on the stage
or up by the fence
today though
he's down by the landwash
watching the object
in the water
his stance is important
it's a manly stance
he has to look manly
this is a moment
that will be long talked about

he'll stand tall years from now
hip angled
and talk about this
but never ever mention
his boy's broken heart

The third child stands
a little to the right
she has dark short cropped hair
a dark sweater and light skirt
her hands are held
behind her back
her feet wide apart
she is rooted and resolute
she has eyes fixed
on three spaces for windows
on the object
in the water
three dark empty spaces
staring back
at three children standing
fixed in this instant
not knowing
not understanding
telling us all
by their stance...

Watching the men
in the boats
fastening the ropes
around the object
tying the knots
shouting orders
starting the engines
getting ready
to move the house
out of the harbour
the house with three
dark windows glaring at us
being towed away
leaving three children
on the landwash
looking, presently,
at an empty harbour

❧

Gaultois Girls are Dancing

for Suzanne and Bob – shipmates, summer 1998

Down in the harbour
of this fishing town
I first heard
the sound of their feet.
In the hall on the hill
they whirl and they twirl
their young bodies
keeping time to the beat.

Above the harbour
of this dwindling town
I first saw
their eyes and their hair.
In the hall on the hill
they swing and they sing
their young hearts
in rhyme with the beat.

All 'round the harbour
of this dying town
I first felt
the death of the bay.
But in the hall on the hill
where they dance and they swing
young children
beat down the ol' way.

❧

November 10 — Armistice Eve

My rooftop deck overlooks
the Newfoundland War Memorial
where young boys on skateboards—
boys of the age
a previous generation
sent to slaughter—
keep their nightly vigil.
Sounds of skateboard wheels spinning
over the edges of solid steps
crack of the board
on concrete
like short bursts
of staccato gunfire
in the otherwise
silent night.
They linger long
under a foggy moon
at play
—boys at play
on the monument—
with boys who lie dead
somewhere.

Tomorrow
a handful of old men

will take time to remember
as they gather in November cold
to weep for fallen comrades.
A bitter wind off the harbour
will make them
pee in their pants
but they'll wear brave faces
as drums beat
prayers are said
the enemy is forgiven
the parade moves on....

On my rooftop deck
under misty stars
I look up
at a hazy hunter's moon
thinking of tomorrow
when a woman
dear to me
arrives from her home
near the Danish border.

Danish Gypsy Princess

There was no indecision in Denmark last night—
where poor Hamlet suffered through his moods—
when I dove into the Gamal Dansk
to bid farewell to Hannah
and to listen
to her stories.
Hannah's maternal grandmother
was a great Danish actress
who courted a stage star
whom she never married
but she bore his child
who bore Hannah.
Hannah tried to love her grandmother
but she was a bitch
giddy for applause
and the roar of the crowd
she missed the blue beauty
in the sky child's eyes
and the warmth of a hungry heart.
Hannah told me all this
one night in Klapenbourg
when we talked long
after my wife and her husband
were sleeping—
talked as we had done
many times before.

Hannah's paternal grandmother
was a Jew
beautiful, married, but childless—
not by choice—
she was determined
to have children
and with her husband's
graceful consent
she sought out
the finest Jewish youths
of Europe
and in Vienna
she made love to a man
who fulfilled her dream
and she bore
Hannah's father
and kept the blood pure.
I know all this
because Hannah told me so
with a mixture of pride and delight
and a little sadness.
When I look in Hannah's eyes
and into the deep blue
of her daughter's
I see all the anguish
of Europe
its pain, its love
and its beauty.

I know—and it's well I know—
because in all these long nights
I talked with Hannah
she told me so...
and more
so much more....
but that's another time
and perhaps
another telling.

❧

Alexandra — Daughter for Me

A tall mountain man
mad
mad as a hatter
stopped me on the narrow road
he said
"You are my friend"

With a flower in his buttonhole
a beanie hauled down around
his skull, a cap on top of that,
his business suit
and his field boots

And this is Alexandra
daughter for me

In his little farm home
with charming Greek fireplace
like those you see in postcards
we ate
raisins in sauce
warm goat's milk with bread
potatoes fried and
wine, walnuts
and coffee served
in dainty cups

The fire was lit
and by it sat
a man—a rather small man—
who had come in from the fields
he was served bread
by Alexandra
fried in olive oil
and he drank Suma
glass after glass
My lovely friend
a German lady
brought a book
and in time we talked
to one another
Spiros (the man)
Alexandra his daughter

We laughed and sang
and shared food and wine together
and when we left to say goodbye
Alexandra followed us out the door
and said Adieu a thousand times
each time differently

Tonight
we saw the grandfather
perform

he looked like a happy Newfoundlander
in his rubber boots
proudly dancing
on the tavern floor
The proud Athenian
danced with her lover
such grace I have not seen
and the eyes of her children
looked on in approval

The old man
after hours of persuasion
leapt onto the floor
and danced
as if it were made for his rhythm
his feet barely moved
as music came
oozing from the boards
fingers began to click
feet began their stomps
the dance glowed
in his face and eyes

In the mountain tonight
another old man lies asleep
thinking of his days
as jeep driver in Morocco
during the war

In the room nearby
Alexandra—
a daughter for me—
lies restless on her bed
thinking of her rich sister
who did so well
in Australia

❧

Poet's Daughter

A great lovely sun
came rising over
the St. John's morning sky

Your father sat singing
with your mother
in lovely harmony

and I sat like a dumb stranger
wondering what other blessings
besides your beauty
that this day held.

Who Will Sing for Me?

(a poem for Shanawdithit)

Poor child
wherever you lie
headless
in the ground
my heart bleeds for you.

Yesterday
I visited
the memorial
erected
supposedly for you.

But it
commemorates
the local parish church
the Church of England
not you.

Your skull was blown to bits
in London
your remains were bulldozed
in St. John's
out of the ground
your bones lost
to make way

for railroad tracks and trains
that run no more
the last of your race
and we
    —the Church of England—
lost your body.

We can create poems and songs
for you
forever more
but we'll never
ever
make up for
what we have done.

If there is a green hill
far away
let it be yours
all yours
and yours alone
let birds sing to you
day and night
forever and forever.

Mission to China

When one of the chosen
could not make it
I was asked to go.

Landing in Beijing
I encountered my first crisis:
lost luggage.
It took a whole day
but with the capable guidance
and soft commands
of the mission's official guide
Wu Jen
we got the luggage back.

At daybreak next morning
I walked outside my hotel
to witness a silent army
of workers pedalling
down the wide street
on bicycles so close together
—going so fast—
they sucked the air
from where I was standing
leaving me in a vacuum
of disbelief.

I felt the same sense
of disbelief
as I struggled
to a prime vantage point
on the Great Wall.
Only from outer space
can the length and breadth
of this backbreaking miracle
be fully seen.

From where I stood
I thought I could hear
their cries of agony
as they lifted heavy stones
held in the hollow
of their stomachs
encircled by bony arms
and lean shoulders.

As they slaved
they must have wondered
whose vision was this
to build a wall to the stars
across mountain peaks
shutting out the light
of the rest of mankind.

In Xian
I stood amazed
looking down in the uncovered earth
to see a clay army of soldiers
and generals on horseback
and thousands more with their weaponry
all created by the whim
of a powerful emperor
who sought the security elsewhere
that he had enjoyed on earth.

Those artists and artisans
whose gifted hands moulded and shaped
this great clay army in the ground
what must they have thought
as they laboured in the mud?
What light guided them?

Now we come to the time
of the sparrows
when the birds
the people are told
have to be driven from the land
because they endanger the crops.
Those who question or resist
are jailed or sent
to labour camps
like my companion for lunch

in Shanghai
who told me his story:
they came and got him in the night
burned his books
destroyed his piano
put him to work
pickaxe, shovel and wheelbarrow
away from his editor's desk.

I kept looking at his hands
—so much like my father's—
fingers like talons
hands curved and calloused.
Amazing that ten years in a pit
in China
wheeling heavy stones
can create a pair of hands
like a fisherman's
across the sea
who spent his life
hauling gear in over the gunwale.
Our mission ended
in Quangzhou
I was asked to give
the farewell words
—the big boys from Beijing
had come down
for the evening—

Wu Jen was nervous
she had to translate
simultaneously.
Over the two weeks
on buses, planes and trains
I got to know her
told her many stories
from Newfoundland.
She told me hers
and we sometimes cried.
Don't be nervous I said
we'll tell stories together tonight
when I want you to speak
I'll nudge you
and you do the same for me.

So we began
in the large crowded restaurant
gently nudging our way
through our thoughts.
You could hear a pin drop.
When we finished there was silence
then applause
and people stood up.
The big man from Beijing
pulled a handkerchief
from his pocket
to wipe the tears away

—that man from Newfoundland
is a poet—
he was heard to say.
He was wrong
I made up the speech
but the poet was Wu Jen
the nervous Chinese woman
who nudged me through it all.

Lesson from Larry

Sometime after we wept
in Bologna for those killed
by a senseless bomb
and again sometime
after we sang on the Italian train
"Abide with Me"
to Don Snowdon
who died
in India
you said to me as the countryside swept by:

"Culture, my friend, is not found
in the galleries of Florence
nor in the museums of Rome
it's that man out there
in the henhouse
with the wheelbarrow and his chicks."

What other way to gauge
the cultural impulse of a nation?

❧

On the Beaches of France

for Gerry Squires

I

At precisely seven o'clock
in the town square
of Saintes
just around the corner
from where the Germans
murdered the Jews
the bells began.

They rang inside my skull
their resonance charmed my bones
and I stood there
terrified
almost as if the firing squad
cocked their guns for me.

All over France
the bells sounded
and in my mind
I heard them clang
from the Anglican church
in my home in Newfoundland.

No one could choose but listen
then I thought of my companion

who stood in equal terror
unable to speak
and I could see
Change Islands in his mind
as the bells clanged
and we stood in the square
innocent victims
of their charm....

II

Where the saltwater rolled in
you could still see
remnants of war
ugly structures embedded
in a beautiful beach.
I could not drink to them
nor toast their health.
I just felt sorry
even embarrassed that they
—who in fact were mine—
came here to fight and bleed
and went home maimed—
while I drank wine
ate bread and loved.
As I thrashed in the waves
of France
my body unencumbered
I had to ask

did they really know
what it felt like to be free?

III

Father spent every night
for a whole week
shining up his old number ten
then it twigged on me
that he was not going in the country
or bird hunting
and I asked the question
to which my child's mind knew the answer.
Father, I said, why have you spent
so much time on the gun?
His answer came slowly
through teary eyes
you'll not understand
but the war is on
and I guess I'll have to go.

IV

When the biggest of the big breakers broke
I threw my arms, legs and chest
unto the top
and I was flung
like a chip unto the sand.
It took me the rest of the day
and many drinks

of Bordeaux and Cognac
to tell my friends
of my epic battle
with the sea
and later on that night
I dreamt the sea
that threw me to the shore
was red
stained with the drops
of father's blood.

Tra Montana

for Luis Zendrera, my friend

On the Eastern Coast
of Spain
north of the tranquil
Bay of Roses
and the Costa Brava
a barren and rocky
point of land
juts out into
the Mediterranean—
it is called
Cap de Creus.

For thousands of years
Cap de Creus
has struck fear into
the hearts of sailors.

North of the Cape
lies the southern end
of the Pyrenees
on the coast of France.
Down over the sharp peaks
of the mountains
come the strong winds
cutting the ridges
like a razor.

Whining, howling,
shrieking, keening,
the wind
funnels its way
southward screeching its way
to the coast
ending its torturous journey exploding
over this bay of wild winds
and smashing into the cliffs of Cap de Creus
like a train
hitting a rock wall
at full speed.

This Northern wind
with all its fury
is called
Tra Montana.

It is not a wind
to meddle with.

Not a single tree
grows on the Cape.

The rocks are pock-marked
with holes blasted
by wind-driven salt
hitting the cliffs
with machine gun power.

Tra Montana
a terror on the Cape.

Tra Montana
a nightmare on the sea.

On the Southern side
in the lund of the cliffs
lie peaceful
calm coves
inlets and islands
that are earthly
Edens.

It is here
Salvador Dali
sought a sanctuary
for his art—
a little cove
on the lund side
within sight
of the fierce Cape.

At the Southern end
of the peninsula
lies Cadaques
a dreamlike haven
sheltered from

the Northern wind—
the harbour entrance
studded with island gems
like Cukcooraku
a granite diamond
set in the peaceful sea.

Tra Montana
your shrieks
and your awesome power
continue to create
widowed hearts
and bring men
to their knees
in full genuflection.

Under the skirts
of your wild beauty
lies Cadaques
a testimony
to man's determination
to create a refuge
in the lee
of nature's terror.

*(Espagna Oct. 6, 1998,
Written in Gaudi Park, Barcelona)*

❦

When it Rains in Puerto Vallarta

for Christopher Pratt

It is a great day for tea
I've had seven cups already.
A world record for me.
Watching the rain pour down
I have a Christopher Pratt view
of the sea from this little cafe
with a straw roof,
a cleanly lined concrete balcony
a set of wooden steps
with finely angled rails
that lead to the beach
in the middle of this portrait.

On the sand
five round plastic tables
each with three chairs
silkscreened in the footprints.
I look through the railings
in the middle of this painting
and see that the third table lies dead
smack in the centre
as if placed there by design—
beyond, at the top of this painting,
is an endless flat sea
so smooth that its millions

of blue, green ripples
are squeejeed perfectly
into an horizonless
grey sky.

This blue green grey morning
is perfect for reading.
The man at the blueclothed table
next to me
is in a wheelchair and is halfway through
a thick book on the Aztecs—
three black birds in procession
crumb-peck their way
along the sand by the tables
and now out of the portrait
a black man with a guitar
strolls through
uncaring for his instrument
where the raindrops scatter
and pitter patter
a fine tune
for his entrance and his exit.

What we have here
is a silkscreen with a difference:
the beach and the balcony
form a proscenium
where the birds, the tour boats

and the rain-walkers
have their moments on stage.
I look up to catch a squadron
of cormorants zoom through
making a black streak
across my painting.
I must leave this spot—the waiter
has just left me another tea—I have set
another world record for drinking—and I must be
off up the beach
to find another art gallery
on this rainy day
in Puerto Vallaerta.

❦

Down Under

North of here the Great Barrier Reef
South Sou'East Tasmania
West Nor'West Alice Springs
and Ayers Rock
all the loveliness beckoning
from a Southern Continent
and I the anxious, curious traveller
wanting to see all

I've come to an abrupt stop
in my travels and my quest
to see the geography of Earth
for here in front of me
neither North nor South
nor East nor West
stands Rachel with her smile
and sweet voice
talking to me
as if I'm the only person
in the Southern world
She shares with me
love of her country
the Sunshine coast
with smiles as broad
as Australia

I drink the white wine
as she speaks

my eyes fixed on hers
her golden ringlets
dangling down her woman's face
teasing on her beauty...
wine in hand
eyes meeting
voices mingling
the afternoon becomes a poem
the whole of Australia
North, South, East and West
stands alluringly,
in front of me...

The lonely heart reaches out,
way out, down under,
a special pain pierces the traveller's quest
geography takes second place
to a lovely woman
who has time for you
time to talk
time to listen
time to be gentle
time to tell you
of her fears, her dreams
time to wish for more
much more of a woman
who is Australia

Padua Woman

She is a woman from Padua
In the evening light
she strolls
white breasted
into the green Jamaican sea
on her return to shore
a red ball of a Caribbean sun
set against a golden grey codfish sky
lights her way to land

I wonder at this beauteous voyage
to and from the sea
would that all voyages
I have known
in Newfoundland
been subject to such splendour
a light in the west
a kind cover of cloud
a beacon of gold to shore
a safe touch of dry land
and
warm soft flesh
until another dawn

Zimbabwe Dancer

Black girl
at the dance club
in Harare
why do you look
so fine?

with gold chains
on your neck
that loop
over pert breasts

and teeth like ivory
of elephant tusks
glistening
through smiling red lips

scent like the delicate flower
I saw above
Devil's Cataract
in Victoria Falls

you flow on the floor
like the Zambezi
slow
silky
warm
as mother's milk

A Maiden from Cape La Hune

My mother from Cape La Hune
lies dying in a home
for aged persons
in Toronto.

She is adored
by a host of children
she bore and raised
who covet her
with self-protected jealousies
but she like a comber
on the Cape rocks
rises above platitudes and schemes
turning the tide of self intent
to flow in favour
of love.

This maiden from Cape La Hune
was my father's choice
for a wife
to bring sons and daughters
into his saltwater life
while fishing the sea.

His young man's eye
caught the sway and swirl

of her dark brown hair
that rolled in rhythm
of long waves
down her shoulders.
His sailor's eye
spotted the movement
of long strands of sea kelp
swaying in the tide
as she flung her lithe body around
on the Saturday night dance floor
in Cape La Hune.

Lusty young fishermen
longed for her
but he won her
with his Fox Island charm.

That was yesterday.
That was a long time ago.
My father is long gone
having made a painful and sudden exit.
She lingers on in a Toronto home
shoved there not by will or wish
but by circumstance—
I said to her
as the contraption holding her body upright
stumbled into the elevator
on the way to supper—

I guess you won't be climbing the tote anymore—
No my son—no more climbs up the hills for me
and no more berry-picking either
and, my dear, I can't write any more letters
my eyes are so bad.

Her words cut me
like a splitting knife.
This is a woman
whose life was letter writing
thousands of words
of love and news
to brothers and sisters
uncles and aunts
cousins and nameless relatives
—this woman
created in Cape La Hune
Sam Baggs's daughter
now come to this...
Caught up in pity for her
I was startled
to hear her voice
as she spoke
to this roomful
of crippled humanity
seated lifeless in the dining room:

This is my son
from Newfoundland
he never backanswered me
in all his life—
no never once
did he
backanswer me.

From up the Shore

for Sarah

He was far from land
in his boat
alone

His heart was lonely
it ached for love

The sea was still
oily smooth

Not a breath of wind
not a ripple
on the water

The sun warm
in a hazy sky
a grey, seal skin
grey sky

His hand was on
the tiller
he had done his work
caught his fish
his boat was full
but his heart was empty

I will rest
he said
before I return
to the empty house

He closed his eyes
as a gentle puff
of wind from
the Nord East
rocked his boat
and swayed him
to sleep.
The wind picked up
it swirled and
twisted around
his craft

From the spume
of saltwater
a form emerged
slithering and sliding
in over the
gunwale and
seated herself
on the tawt—
he opened his eyes

I am your woman
daughter of the sea
I was created
to love you
and I have learned
to love you
while you've been out here
on the saltwater
I want to be
with you and comfort you
until you die

Take me to shore
to your empty home
and I will fill it
with love

I will care for you
and be there
with you
to the end...
In return
you must promise
not to speak
of how and where we met.
You will say
I came from
up the shore

somewhere...
and that is true
somewhere
I came from somewhere
and people will wonder
but never know
where.
It will not matter
they do not know
as long as
I care for you
and love you

And that
I will do

He rowed to shore
with an easy heart.
A crowd gathered
on the wharf
to view his
strange companion

From up the shore
says one, I s'pose
No one up the shore
I knows
says another

Well b'y she got to be
from somewhere
I allow he didn't get her
on his jigger.
He grinned and
she smiled
as they laughed
Everything was all right
the woman
from somewhere
had come home
making her entrance
on a tide of laughter

What shall I call you
he said
She was silent for a moment
and then softly she said
call me—Sarah
Yes, call me Sarah

Young Dobbin the Diver

These words are for you
my old saltwater friend
the man who shared with me
the cold of a northern
Newfoundland winter
when journeys to the bottom
were not well known

Was it down my throat or yours
the dark rum was poured
by a veteran of the ice
who knew better than most
the agony of cold
and the crippled clutch
of a lone heart
caught in the winter wind?

And who will understand
your laughter
defiant as the gaggling
seagull on the wing
tormenting our human
frailty with your
stubborn song of joy

Who will ever know
your fine spoken metaphor of life?

Who would ever dare
take the journeys into depths
that you have gone
and who would ever seek
the bottom of your love?

You probably reached out
when none was there
reaching for a hand
a touch
a little balance—
in this ruckus
between life and death

We were not there
at that moment—
but just as well—
the old diver on the bottom
knows that when it's up it's up
when it's down it's down
and we don't mistake the signals

So farewell old friend
young Dobbin the diver
farewell and then again
farewell.

The Happiness Equation

The music will roll on
under the hills
by the sea
when you are gone
old lovers
will tell their tales
of love
and look for
a welcoming twinkle
in the eyes
of the listeners
old fools wise fools
know that
happiness
is an equation
a secret balance
between
passion and tolerance
and you my friend
and I
who know all
this
must live with
the reality
that knowing
is being

but knowing helps
in the long lonely
nights—when
passion is absent
from your pillow.

❦

Last Thoughts

for Sarah

Tonight you will lie
in your bed
and wonder if,
—if ever—
you will spend
another night
together.

Love is not
in question
never was
now
or ever shall be
between you.

What we never enter in
never ever enter
in
the formula of love
is
our mortality
it is as if
it were not a factor
though it was
is

and ever shall be
the final factor
in the equation
of love
as is—now—
and ever shall be.

❦

How Does Your Garden Grow?

for Mary

Grandfather knew what he was doing
when he built a fence
around your flower garden
that you made as a child
in our dear place of birth—
Fox Island.

Grandfather knew things about beauty
working a lifetime on the sea
and living his years
raising a family
in a home on an island
surrounded by saltwater.

Grandfather knew many things
about winds, tides, heavy seas,
fog, sunkers and danger
that lurks
in the shadows
that swiftly destroys
our delicate efforts to preserve beauty.

Grandfather must have chuckled
to see you there in your garden
shooshing the hens away

from your blossoming flowers
and he must have taken delight
in his love for you
as with hammer, saw and nails
he built a little fence
to keep the bothersome hens
out of the growing beauty spot.

Grandfather knew
in his fine old saltwater wisdom
that no matter how hard you try
things do not last
no, not even tough, careful old fishermen
that know the weather and sea—
they go down
and so do little fences
built to protect
a child's flower garden
these too fall to the ground.

But Grandfather knew
that it was important to build
a little wall
around a spot of beauty
much like loving arms
you put around
a son or daughter
a sister or brother

a mother or father
a husband or wife
an aunt or an uncle
a niece or nephew
or a cousin
the arms are there
like a fence of love.

But Grandfather would not
have known
that his great grand-daughter
today
picked up a basket of flowers
went to the chapel to pray
then took her bundle of beauty
to his grand-daughter
—the flower garden child—
bound to a bed
in the Massachusetts General Hospital
with tubes feeding her antibiotics
wires recording
her electronic heartbeats.

Grandfather would be pleased though
that his fence and the garden
of beautiful marigolds
daisies and buttercups
would never die

that a child's rhyme
by a flower child
will forever be sung.

Mary, Mary
quite contrary
how does your garden grow
with marigolds and daisies
and buttercups
all in a row?

❦

Morning in Bologna

for Al

On this Spring afternoon
the Piazza Maggiora sings
with life: young men romp
in the square: old men rant
and shout at one another wildly
proclaiming each other's right to be right.

A cathedral sits solid and silent
on one end; while on the other
brisk with business and in glorious sunshine
a cluster of cafés pours forth
cappuccino, espresso, beer and vino
to lovers, travellers and the curious.

Long legged olive skinned women
strut their youthful way
through torrid glances
across the square;
Italy comes alive.
Pigeons flutter in exultation;
old men octave their voices
to a higher pitch in argument
young men flex their limbs
and play poetry with a pig's bladder

bouncing the ball on head, knee and toe
while their eyes, like shafts of fire,
fix on the moving madrigals
that slide their sultry, directionless
ways through the crowd.

My mind winds its way
back in time
to a little room
on the Via Independenza
in the Majestic Bagliona
where my friend, a poet, and I
sat all night long
reading verses to one another.
At dawn an old man came
down the street:
he was the first alive that morning
and we watched him stretch and yawn
glance up at the old cathedral
then bending
unlocked
the door of his shop
ready for the day's business.
Above him in our room
across the street
we felt like two gods
watching, smiling on the man below.

Our day-long night
rolled into one
come too soon to an end
while his long day
had just begun.

❧

Lines from Oporto

Between me and the setting sun
there is a jagged ridge of rocks
a rolling surf
a sandy beach.
For the past hour
a man dressed in black
wearing a tam
has darted catlike
back and forth
across the ridge
heaving his baited hooks
into the Atlantic.

He disappears momentarily
and if I do not watch him
—every moment
I lose sight of him
as he becomes
in a crouch
a part of the reef
oblivious to me and my concerns.

How long he'll stay I do not know
but my wine is gone—
the sun has just taken the light away
he's disappeared again
and I'm left between sea and sand

sitting on a rock,
shivering my way into the night.
Just as I'm about to leave
my perch of rocks
on the beach
I see over my right shoulder
a woman
in a black shawl
black sweater and skirt
barefooted
gathering kelp
at the edge of the tide.

She shoves it in a twine basket
at her waist
and carries it to the beachtop
to dry.
At every tide she will come
as her mound of kelp
will grow and dry in the sun
covered over by straw and rocks bound
down with rope.

Old woman you do not know
I know nothing of you
except we share this sandy beach
these dark rocks
the setting sun
and this kelp.

Burgeo Girls Don't Cry

Burgeo girls
don't cry
you can fire snowballs
at them
stand them up
at the garden gate
but there's never
ever
a tear in the eye
but that's because
we can't see
their hearts
which like winter moons
sit like silver
in a dark blue sky
shining their light
on a frosty night
hiding from us
the black tearducts
of the universe.

So you, my sister,
at this time
of your mortal peril
will shine
like the flower

you always were
at the garden gate
on one side
life, light and laughter
on the other
who knows
but who cares

Burgeo girls don't cry
—no matter what—
          never did

                    never will.

❧

For a Californian Maiden

Not every maiden
from California—or from anywhere
is welcomed to my shore.

The Sou'West Coast
of Newfoundland
extends a wary eye
to newcomers.

Even those accompanied
by native sons.

This awesome coast
with its leaning cliffs
endless fjords
and pounding seas
is a jealous lover —
tumultuous, clinging,
possessive...
dangerous.

You came through
all of it
the heavy seas of passion,
tension and emotion—

your tranquility
—a feather on the ocean—
in company of three raging bulls.
One who honoured you
another who saw the need
for you
and the third
a Sou'West Coast man
who wanted to share
the beauty of his land
with a Californian maiden.

Snake Lightning

When the snake lightning strikes
flashing its venomous strokes
across the sky—
you can cuddle up to me
and rest your fear.
During the most terrifying moments
that cause you to tremble
I shall sing old songs from my island country—
songs of roaming and longing,
of sailors far from home,
of lovely maidens
caught in love's embrace
of Rachel faithful
to her lover...

And dawn will come
all too quickly
the morning sun will rise too soon
and all the forked lightning
of the night
and all the images of twirling snakes
will give way to the sweet smells
of roses made wet
by the night's rain
and the fresh fragrance
of a lover's heat.

❧

Christ in the Pizza Place

for Al Pittman

The steamy Naples night stinks
of degradation—
male whores, prostitutes,
garbage and piss fill
every alley.
This Roman decadence
seemingly a long way from
my Grade IX Latin textbook.
But the ancient craftsmen
built well
and their stone works remain
for boys with a soccer ball
to bounce their skills
off the walls and cobblestones
while defying
the crazy Italian traffic.

Now you ol' friend and poet
cut into my mind
as I stopped by this place
on the corner.
For what I saw
I chose to enter.
My Air Canada "En Route"
experience said

avoid this slum
but my Newfoundland upbringing
told me to take a seat.
This place is as places go
no bigger than a stagehead
but set on the corner
as it is
it hums with industry.
A large Italian tiled kiln
burns in the corner
the hard wood
and shavings throw off
a pure blue flame.
To the left, high on the wall
is a plaster sculpture
of Christ, a blue fluorescent
halo surrounding Him and on
the lace covered shelf
at His feet are three
vases of flowers—
red carnations in the middle
and violets on either side.

My pizza tastes
like homemade bread
toasted on the kitchen stove
and the wine has
a fragrance

and a taste that challenge
Ovidian metaphors.

I must be a strange sight
to the pizza-maker
a grey old man
with a curled moustache,
standing below
the blue haloed Christ
diligently making his pizzas
passing them to the man at the oven
who with his paddle shoves them
into the blue flame,
to see me writing words
on an envelope
to a Placentia Bay poet.

I feel it strange too.
I know there are ten million
other things to do
but somehow the irony
of the moment touched me
and you filled all my world.

I mean, look at this
fucking place—the first
glance screams out
its message:

"Head for the Hilton!"
But the pizza place
is the holding centre—
the old man works his skills;
the man at the oven delights
in his fire browned bread;
and the boy serving
the checkered clothed tables
whistles and sprints around.
Behind the rough exterior
the blue flame burns pure;
the old man creates his forms;
the boy voices his love of work
and Christ is properly
administered to on the wall.
And I am graced
with kindness
as long minutes
after paying my bill
the boy returns,
refills my glass and says
for you, Signor
the eyes of the pizza-maker twinkle
the man at the oven smiles
I raise my glass
and to you—my friends.

֍

You Asked for a Poem

for Maureen and Tess

On some starry night
when I'm alone
I wander out to hear
the night winds
sing to me.
A choral cacophony
twirls down
the Gros Morne canyons
bursting through
bountiful Bonne Bay
where ocean breezes whip
the sounds around
into lilts and ripples
of night music
that for all the world is like
Irish laughter
out on the bay.